MW00613914

Count Your Blessings
100 BLESSINGS A Day

by
Rabbi Ron Isaacs

KTAV Publishing House, Inc.
Jersey City, NJ 07306

Library of Congress Cataloging-in-Publication Data

Isaacs, Ron.
  Count your blessing : 100 blessings a day / by Ron Isaacs.
    p. cm.
  Includes bibliographical refernces and index.
  ISBN 0-88125-846-6
  1. Judaism--Prayer-book and devotions
    --English. 2. Judaism--Liturgy. I. Title.
  BM665.I83 2004
  296.7--dc22

                                    2004014885

                  Published by
          KTAV Publishing House, Inc.
              930 Newark Avenue
             Jersey City, NJ 07306
            Email: info@ktav.com
                  www.ktav.com
                (201) 963-9524
               Fax (201) 963-0102

Contents

Introduction

The building block of all Jewish prayer is the blessing. The blessings pronounced on various occasions are attributed to the Men of the Great Assembly (400–300 BCE), the spiritual leaders in the time of Ezra the Scribe. Blessings were formulated for practically every contingency: for the usual experiences of daily life, such as arising from sleep, dressing, eating, and drinking, and for the unusual happenings, such as escaping from danger, recovering from illness, or seeing something wondrous in nature.

The Hebrew word for blessing, *beracha*, is generally understood to be derived from the Hebrew word *berech* ("knee"). The bending of the knee while praying was one of the ways of honoring God. The Rashba, a Talmudic scholar, has said that the word *beracha* is derived from the Hebrew word *bereicha* which means a spring of water. Just as a spring flows constantly and its waters increase, so, too, when we bless God we are proclaiming our desire to display God's every-increasing presence in the world.

Living life as a Jew is a magnificent gift. Judaism teaches us to mark our time by saying blessings. What is a blessing? A blessing is anything that begins with these six words:

> *Baruch ata Adonai Elohenu melech ha'olam...*
> *Praised are You, Adonai our God, Ruler of the Universe...*

There are shorter forms of the blessing that simply begin *Baruch ata Adonai—Praised are You, God.* The longest form of a blessing is that which is recited in conjunction with the performance of a specific religious obligation (*mitzvah*). It adds the phrase *asher kidshanu bemitzvotav vetzivanu*—who sanctified us with mitzvot and commanded us to…"

Each moment of our lives counts. The Jewish practice of saying blessings each day derives from the desire to promote joy and appreciation, wonder and thankfulness, amazement and praise. By noticing our gifts in life each day, we are striving for a place of holiness.

From Bible times to the present, Jews have used blessings to consecrate the special moments of our lives. Rabbi Meir, one of the great Talmudic sages of his day, used to say: "A person should say one hundred blessings daily" (Talmud, *Menachot* 43B). According to Rabbi Meir, saying one hundred blessings a day will help you to master the virtue of awe and reverence. If each of us each day were to take notice of 100 things in our lives, we would be much more sensitive to everything going on around us.

I invite each of you to take notice of what's happening around you. You are encouraged to carry this little book of blessings with you. Look for blessing opportunities, and take some time to pause and say a blessing. Saying blessings will help teach you to truly notice what is going on around you, and show appreciation for it. May each of you count your 100 blessings each day!

RABBI RON ISAACS

Upon Awakening in the Morning

1.

בָּרוּךְ אַתָּה יְיָ אֱלֹהֵינוּ מֶלֶךְ הָעוֹלָם אֲשֶׁר קִדְּשָׁנוּ
בְּמִצְוֹתָיו, וְצִוָּנוּ עַל נְטִילַת יָדָיִם:

Baruch ata Adonai Elohenu melech ha'olam asher kidshanu bemitzvotav vetzivanu al netilat yadayim.

Praised are You, Adonai our God, Ruler of the Universe, who has made us holy with mitzvot and instructed us to wash our hands.

Preparing to Pray

ﬞﺵ DONNING A TALLIT

2.

בָּרוּךְ אַתָּה יְיָ אֱלֹהֵינוּ מֶלֶךְ הָעוֹלָם אֲשֶׁר קִדְּשָׁנוּ בְּמִצְוֹתָיו, וְצִוָּנוּ לְהִתְעַטֵּף בַּצִּיצִת.

Baruch ata Adonai Elohenu melech ha'olam asher kidshanu bemitzvotav vetzivanu le'hitatef ba'tzitzit.

Praised are You, Adonai our God, Ruler of the Universe, who has made us holy with mitzvot and instructed us to wrap ourselves with fringes.

⁪ DONNING TEFILLIN

When putting on the *tefillin shel yad* (hand tefillin)

3.

בָּרוּךְ אַתָּה יְיָ אֱלֹהֵינוּ מֶלֶךְ הָעוֹלָם, אֲשֶׁר קִדְּשָׁנוּ
בְּמִצְוֹתָיו וְצִוָּנוּ לְהָנִיחַ תְּפִלִּין.

*Baruch ata Adonai Elohenu melech ha'olam asher
kidshanu bemitzvotav vetzivanu lehani'ach tefillin.*

Praised are You, Adonai our God, Ruler of the
Universe, who has made us holy with mitzvot and
instructed us to wear tefillin.

4.

בָּרוּךְ אַתָּה יְיָ אֱלֹהֵינוּ מֶלֶךְ הָעוֹלָם, אֲשֶׁר קִדְּשָׁנוּ
בְּמִצְוֹתָיו, וְצִוָּנוּ עַל מִצְוַת תְּפִלִּין.

Baruch ata Adonai Elohenu melech ha'olam asher kidshanu bemitzvotav vetzivanu al mitzvat tefillin.

Praised are You, Adonai our God, Ruler of the Universe, who has made us holy with mitzvot and instructed us concerning the precept of tefillin.

On Studying and grateful
for the gift of Torah

5.

בָּרוּךְ אַתָּה יְיָ אֱלֹהֵינוּ מֶלֶךְ הָעוֹלָם, אֲשֶׁר קִדְּשָׁנוּ
בְּמִצְוֹתָיו, וְצִוָּנוּ לַעֲסוֹק בְּדִבְרֵי תוֹרָה:

*Baruch ata Adonai Elohenu melech ha'olam asher
kidshanu bemitzvotav vetzivanu la'asok bedivray
Torah.*

Praised are You, Adonai our God, Ruler of the
Universe, whose mitzvot add holiness to our lives
and who gave us the mitzvah to study words of
Torah.

6.

בָּרוּךְ אַתָּה יְיָ, הַמַּחֲזִיר נְשָׁמוֹת לִפְגָרִים מֵתִים.

Baruch ata Adonai hamachazir neshamot leefgareem mayteem.

Praised are You, Adonai, who restores the soul to the lifeless, exhausted body.

16.

בָּרוּךְ אַתָּה יְיָ אֱלֹהֵינוּ מֶלֶךְ הָעוֹלָם, שֶׁעָשָׂה לִי כָּל צָרְכִּי:

Baruch ata Adonai Elohenu melech ha'olam she'asah lee kol tzorkee.

Praised are You, Adonai our God, Ruler of the Universe, who provides me with everything.

17.

בָּרוּךְ אַתָּה יְיָ אֱלֹהֵינוּ מֶלֶךְ הָעוֹלָם הַמֵּכִין מִצְעֲדֵי גָבֶר:

Baruch ata Adonai Elohenu melech ha'olam ha-maycheen meetzaday gaver.

Praised are You, Adonai our God, Ruler of the Universe, who guides us on our path.

14.

בָּרוּךְ אַתָּה יְיָ אֱלֹהֵינוּ מֶלֶךְ הָעוֹלָם, זוֹקֵף כְּפוּפִים:

Baruch ata Adonai Elohenu melech ha'olam zokef kefufeem.

Praised are You, Adonai our God, Ruler of the Universe, who raises the downtrodden.

15.

בָּרוּךְ אַתָּה יְיָ אֱלֹהֵינוּ מֶלֶךְ הָעוֹלָם, רוֹקַע הָאָרֶץ עַל הַמָּיִם:

Praised are You, Adonai our God, Ruler of the Universe, who creates heaven and earth.

12.

בָּרוּךְ אַתָּה יְיָ אֱלֹהֵינוּ מֶלֶךְ הָעוֹלָם, מַלְבִּישׁ
עֲרֻמִּים:

Baruch ata Adonai Elohenu melech ha'olam malbeesh arumeem.

Praised are You, Adonai our God, Ruler of the Universe, who clothes the naked.

13.

בָּרוּךְ אַתָּה יְיָ אֱלֹהֵינוּ מֶלֶךְ הָעוֹלָם, מַתִּיר
אֲסוּרִים:

Baruch ata Adonai Elohenu melech ha'olam mateer asureem.

Praised are You, Adonai our God, Ruler of the Universe, who releases the imprisoned.

10.

בָּרוּךְ אַתָּה יְיָ אֱלֹהֵינוּ מֶלֶךְ הָעוֹלָם, שֶׁעָשַׂנִי בֶּן־ (בַּת־) חוֹרִין:

Baruch ata Adonai Elohenu melech ha'olam she'asanee ben (f. bat) choreen.

Praised are You, Adonai our God, Ruler of the Universe, who has made me a free person.

11.

בָּרוּךְ אַתָּה יְיָ אֱלֹהֵינוּ מֶלֶךְ הָעוֹלָם, פּוֹקֵחַ עִוְרִים:

Baruch ata Adonai Elohenu melech ha'olam poke'ach eevreem.

Praised are You, Adonai our God, Ruler of the Universe, who gives sight to blind people.

8.

בָּרוּךְ אַתָּה יְיָ אֱלֹהֵינוּ מֶלֶךְ הָעוֹלָם, שֶׁעָשַׂנִי
בְּצַלְמוֹ:

*Baruch ata Adonai Elohenu melech ha'olam
she'asanee betzalmo.*

Praised are You, Adonai our God, Ruler of the
Universe, who has made me in God's image.

9.

בָּרוּךְ אַתָּה יְיָ אֱלֹהֵינוּ מֶלֶךְ הָעוֹלָם, שֶׁעָשַׂנִי
יִשְׂרָאֵל:

*Baruch ata Adonai Elohenu melech ha'olam
she'asanee yisrael.*

Praised are You, Adonai our God, Ruler of the
Universe, who has made me a Jew.

In the Prayerbook

7.

בָּרוּךְ אַתָּה יְיָ אֱלֹהֵינוּ מֶלֶךְ הָעוֹלָם, אֲשֶׁר נָתַן
לַשֶּׂכְוִי בִינָה, לְהַבְחִין בֵּין יוֹם וּבֵין לַיְלָה:

*Baruch ata Adonai Elohenu melech ha'olam asher
natan le'sechvee veena le-havecheen bayn yom
u'vayn laila.*

Praised are You, Adonai our God, Ruler of the
Universe who helps Your creatures distinguish
day and night.

18.

בָּרוּךְ אַתָּה יְיָ אֱלֹהֵינוּ מֶלֶךְ הָעוֹלָם, אוֹזֵר יִשְׂרָאֵל
בִּגְבוּרָה:

Baruch ata Adonai Elohenu melech ha'olam ozer yisrael beegevurah.

Praised are You, Adonai our God, Ruler of the Universe, who strengthens Israel with courage.

19.

בָּרוּךְ אַתָּה יְיָ אֱלֹהֵינוּ מֶלֶךְ הָעוֹלָם, עוֹטֵר יִשְׂרָאֵל
בְּתִפְאָרָה:

Baruch ata Adonai Elohenu melech ha'olam oter yisrael be-teefarah.

Praised are You, Adonai our God, Ruler of the Universe, who gives Israel glory.

20.

בָּרוּךְ אַתָּה יְיָ אֱלֹהֵינוּ מֶלֶךְ הָעוֹלָם, הַנּוֹתֵן לַיָּעֵף
כֹּחַ:

Baruch ata Adonai Elohenu melech ha'olam ha'noten le'ya'ef koach.

Praised are You, Adonai our God, Ruler of the Universe, who restores strength to those who are tired.

21.

בָּרוּךְ אַתָּה יְיָ אֱלֹהֵינוּ מֶלֶךְ הָעוֹלָם, הַמַּעֲבִיר שֵׁנָה
מֵעֵינָי וּתְנוּמָה מֵעַפְעַפָּי:

Baruch ata Adonai Elohenu melech ha'olam ha'ma'aveer shayna may'ayneye u'tenumah may'afapeye.

Praised are You, Adonai our God, Ruler of the universe, who removes sleep from my eyes and slumber from my eyelids.

22.

בָּרוּךְ אַתָּה יְיָ, גּוֹמֵל חֲסָדִים טוֹבִים לְעַמּוֹ יִשְׂרָאֵל:

Baruch ata Adonai gomel chasadim tovim l'amo yisrael.

Praised are You, Adonai, who bestows lovingkindness upon His people Israel.

☙ APPRECIATING GOD'S HOLINESS

23.

בָּרוּךְ אַתָּה יְיָ, מְקַדֵּשׁ אֶת שִׁמְךָ בָּרַבִּים:

Baruch ata Adonai me'kadesh et sheemcha barabeem.

Praised are You, Adonai, who manifests holiness to all humanity.

24.

בָּרוּךְ אַתָּה יְיָ, מֶלֶךְ מְהֻלָּל בַּתִּשְׁבָּחוֹת:

Barcuh ata Adonai melech me'hulal ba'tishbachot.

Praised are You, Adonai, Ruler extolled with songs of praise.

25.

בָּרוּךְ אַתָּה יְיָ, אֵל מֶלֶךְ גָּדוֹל בַּתִּשְׁבָּחוֹת, אֵל הַהוֹדָאוֹת, אֲדוֹן הַנִּפְלָאוֹת, הַבּוֹחֵר בְּשִׁירֵי זִמְרָה, מֶלֶךְ, אֵל, חֵי הָעוֹלָמִים.

Baruch ata Adonai El melech gadol bateeshbachot El ha'hoda'ot Adon ha-neefla'ot habocher besheeray zimrah melech El chai ha'olameem.

Praised are you, Sovereign of wonders, crowned with adoration, delighting in mortal song and psalm, exalted Ruler, eternal life of the universe.

26.

בָּרוּךְ אַתָּה יְיָ, אֱלֹהֵינוּ מֶלֶךְ הָעוֹלָם, יוֹצֵר אוֹר,
וּבוֹרֵא חְשֶׁךְ, עֹשֶׂה שָׁלוֹם וּבוֹרֵא אֶת הַכֹּל:

*Baruch ata Adonai Elohenu melech ha'olam yotzer
ohr u'voray choshech oseh shalom u'voray et hakol.*

Praised are You, Adonai our God, Ruler of the
Universe, creating light and fashioning darkness,
ordaining the order of all creation.

❧ PRAISING GOD FOR CREATING LIGHTS OF
THE UNIVERSE

27.

בָּרוּךְ אַתָּה יְיָ יוֹצֵר הַמְּאוֹרוֹת:

Baruch ata Adonai yotzer ha'me'orote.

Praised are You, Adonai, Creator of lights.

28.

בָּרוּךְ אַתָּה יְיָ, הַבּוֹחֵר בְּעַמּוֹ יִשְׂרָאֵל בְּאַהֲבָה.

Baruch ata Adonai ha-bocher be'amo yisrael be'ahavah.

Praised are You, Adonai, who chooses His people Israel in love.

29.

בָּרוּךְ אַתָּה יְיָ גָּאַל יִשְׂרָאֵל:

Baruch ata Adonai ga'al yisrael.

Praised are You, Adonai, Redeemer of the people Israel.

Blessings of the Amidah

❧ PRAISING GOD FOR BEING ABRAHAM'S SHIELD

30.

בָּרוּךְ אַתָּה יְיָ, מָגֵן אַבְרָהָם:

Baruch ata Adonai magen Avraham.

Praised are You, Adonai, Shield of Abraham.

❧ PRAISING GOD FOR IMMORTALITY

31.

בָּרוּךְ אַתָּה יְיָ, מְחַיֶּה הַמֵּתִים:

Baruch ata Adonai me'chayay ha-mayteem.

Praised are You, Adonai, who returns the dead to life.

32.

בָּרוּךְ אַתָּה יְיָ, הָאֵל הַקָּדוֹשׁ (בעשי״ת: הַמֶּלֶךְ הַקָּדוֹשׁ).

Baruch ata Adonai ha'El ha-kadosh.

Praised are You, Adonai, holy God.

ప PRAISING GOD FOR GRANTING
INTELLIGENCE

33.

בָּרוּךְ אַתָּה יְיָ, חוֹנֵן הַדָּעַת.

Baruch ata Adonai chonen ha'da'at.

Praised are You, Adonai, who graciously grants
intelligence.

34.

בָּרוּךְ אַתָּה יְיָ, הָרוֹצֶה בִּתְשׁוּבָה.

Baruch ata Adonai ha-rotzeh beeteshuvah.

Praised are You, Adonai, who welcomes repent-
ance.

35.

בָּרוּךְ אַתָּה יְיָ, חַנּוּן הַמַּרְבֶּה לִסְלֹחַ.

Baruch ata Adonai chanun ha-marbeh leeslo'ach.

Praised are You, Adonai, gracious and forgiving
God.

36.

בָּרוּךְ אַתָּה יְיָ, גּוֹאֵל יִשְׂרָאֵל.

Baruch ata Adonai go'el yisrael.

Praised are You, Adonai, Redeemer of the people Israel.

☙ PRAISING GOD FOR ANSWERING THE AFFLICTED

(Recited on fast days)

37.

בָּרוּךְ אַתָּה יְיָ, הָעוֹנֶה בְּעֵת צָרָה.

Baruch ata Adonai ha'oneh be'et tzarah.

Praised are You, Adonai, who answers the afflicted.

44.

בָּרוּךְ אַתָּה יְיָ, בּוֹנֵה יְרוּשָׁלָיִם.

Baruch ata Adonai boneh ye-rushalayim.

Praised are You, Adonai, who builds Jerusalem.

ཚུ PRAISING GOD FOR ASSURING DELIVERANCE

45.

בָּרוּךְ אַתָּה יְיָ, מַצְמִיחַ קֶרֶן יְשׁוּעָה.

Baruch ata Adonai matzmee'ach keren ye-shu'ah.

Praised are You, Adonai, who assures our deliverance.

38.

בָּרוּךְ אַתָּה יְיָ, רוֹפֵא חוֹלֵי עַמוֹ יִשְׂרָאֵל.

Baruch ata Adonai rofay cholay amo yisrael.

Praised are You, Adonai, Healer of the people Israel.

ཚུ PRAISING GOD FOR BLESSING THE YEARS

39.

בָּרוּךְ אַתָּה יְיָ, מְבָרֵךְ הַשָּׁנִים.

Baruch ata Adonai me'varech ha-shaneem.

Praised are You, Adonai, who blesses the years.

PRAISING GOD FOR GATHERING THE DISPERSED

40.

בָּרוּךְ אַתָּה יְיָ, מְקַבֵּץ נִדְחֵי עַמּוֹ יִשְׂרָאֵל.

Baruch ata Adonai me-kabetz needchay amo yisrael.

Praised are You, Adonai, who gathers the dispersed of His people Israel.

PRAISING GOD FOR LOVING JUSTICE

41.

בָּרוּךְ אַתָּה יְיָ, מֶלֶךְ אוֹהֵב צְדָקָה וּמִשְׁפָּט (בעשי״ת: הַמֶּלֶךְ הַמִּשְׁפָּט).

Baruch ata Adonai melech ohev tzedakah u'mishpat.

Praised are You, Adonai, who loves justice.

PRAISING GOD FOR HUMBLING THE ARROGANT

42.

בָּרוּךְ אַתָּה יְיָ, שֹׁבֵר אֹיְבִים וּמַכְנִיעַ זֵדִים.

Baruch ata Adonai shover oyveem u'machneeya zaydeem.

Praised are You, Adonai, who humbles the arrogant.

PRAISING GOD FOR SUSTAINING THE RIGHTEOUS

43.

בָּרוּךְ אַתָּה יְיָ, מִשְׁעָן וּמִבְטָח לַצַּדִּיקִים.

Baruch ata Adonai meeshan u'meevtach la-tzadeekeem.

Praised are You, Adonai, who sustains the righteous.

46.

בָּרוּךְ אַתָּה יְיָ, שׁוֹמֵעַ תְּפִלָּה.

Baruch ata Adonai shomaya tefillah.

Praised are You, Adonai, who hears prayer.

47.

בָּרוּךְ אַתָּה יְיָ, הַמַּחֲזִיר שְׁכִינָתוֹ לְצִיּוֹן.

Baruch ata Adonai ha-machazeer she-cheenato le-tziyon.

Praised are You, Adonai, who restores His presence to Zion.

48.

בָּרוּךְ אַתָּה יְיָ, הַטּוֹב שִׁמְךָ וּלְךָ נָאֶה לְהוֹדוֹת.

Baruch ata Adonai ha-tov sheemcha u-lecha na'eh le'hodote.

Praised are You, Adonai, to whom all praise is due.

☙ PRAISING GOD FOR MAKING PEACE

49.

בָּרוּךְ אַתָּה יְיָ, הַמְבָרֵךְ אֶת עַמּוֹ יִשְׂרָאֵל בַּשָּׁלוֹם.

Baruch ata Adonai ha-mevarech et amo yisrael bashalom.

Praised are You, Adonai, who blesses Israel with peace.

Blessings on Torah Reading Days

First Blessing

50.

בָּרוּךְ אַתָּה יְיָ אֱלֹהֵינוּ מֶלֶךְ הָעוֹלָם, אֲשֶׁר בָּחַר בָּנוּ
מִכָּל הָעַמִּים וְנָתַן לָנוּ אֶת תּוֹרָתוֹ: בָּרוּךְ אַתָּה יְיָ,
נוֹתֵן הַתּוֹרָה:

Baruch ata Adonai Elohenu melech ha'olam asher
bachar banu mikol ha'ameem ve-natan lanu et
torato. Baruch ata Adonai notayn ha-Torah.

Praised are You, Adonai our God, Ruler of the Universe who has chosen us from among all peoples
by giving us His Torah, Praised are You. Adonai,
who gives the Torah.

51.

בָּרוּךְ אַתָּה יְיָ אֱלֹהֵינוּ מֶלֶךְ הָעוֹלָם, אֲשֶׁר נֶתַן לָנוּ
תּוֹרַת אֱמֶת, וְחַיֵּי עוֹלָם נָטַע בְּתוֹכֵנוּ: בָּרוּךְ אַתָּה
יְיָ, נוֹתֵן הַתּוֹרָה:

*Baruch ata Adonai Elohenu melech ha'olam asher
natan lanu torat emet ve-chayei olam natach
betochaynu. Baruch ata Adonai notayn ha-Torah.*

Praised are You, Adonai our God, Ruler of the Universe, who has given us the Torah of truth, planting
within us eternal life. Praised are You, Adonai who
gives the Torah.

Candlelighting Blessings for the Sabbath and Festivals

☙ SHABBAT

52.

בָּרוּךְ אַתָּה יְיָ אֱלֹהֵינוּ מֶלֶךְ הָעוֹלָם, אֲשֶׁר קִדְּשָׁנוּ בְּמִצְוֹתָיו, וְצִוָּנוּ לְהַדְלִיק נֵר שֶׁל שַׁבָּת.

Baruch ata Adonai Elohenu melech ha'olam asher kidshanu bemitzvotav vetzivanu l'hadlik ner shel shabbat.

Praised are You Adonai our God Ruler of the Universe who has made us holy with mitzvot and commanded us to light the Sabbath candles.

✆ FESTIVALS (SUKKOT, SHEMINI ATZERET, PASSOVER AND SHAVUOT)

53.

בָּרוּךְ אַתָּה יְיָ אֱלֹהֵינוּ מֶלֶךְ הָעוֹלָם, אֲשֶׁר קִדְּשָׁנוּ בְּמִצְוֹתָיו, וְצִוָּנוּ לְהַדְלִיק נֵר שֶׁל יוֹם טוֹב.

Baruch ata Adonai Elohenu melech ha'olam asher kidshanu bemitzvotav vetzivanu l'hadlik ner shel yom tov.

Praised are You Adonai our God Ruler of the Universe who has made us holy with mitzvot and commanded us to light the festival candles.

Rosh Hashanah

54.

בָּרוּךְ אַתָּה יְיָ אֱלֹהֵינוּ מֶלֶךְ הָעוֹלָם, אֲשֶׁר קִדְּשָׁנוּ
בְּמִצְוֹתָיו, וְצִוָּנוּ לְהַדְלִיק נֵר שֶׁל (בשבת: שַׁבָּת
וְשֶׁל) יוֹם טוֹב.

*Baruch ata Adonai Elohenu melech ha'olam asher
kidshanu bemitzvotav vetzivanu l'hadlik ner shel (on
Shabbat, add "shel shabbat veshel") yom tov.*

Praised are You Adonai our God Ruler of the
Universe who has made us holy with mitzvot and
commanded us to light the (Shabbat and) festival
candles.

55.

בָּרוּךְ אַתָּה יְיָ אֱלֹהֵינוּ מֶלֶךְ הָעוֹלָם, אֲשֶׁר קִדְּשָׁנוּ בְּמִצְוֹתָיו, וְצִוָּנוּ לִשְׁמוֹעַ קוֹל שׁוֹפָר.

Baruch ata Adonai Elohenu melech ha'olam asher kidshanu bemitzvotav vetzeevanu leeshmo'ah kol shofar.

Praised are You, Adonai our God, Ruler of the Universe, who has made us holy by mitzvot and commanded us concerning the sounding of the shofar.

Yom Kippur

56.

בָּרוּךְ אַתָּה יְיָ אֱלֹהֵינוּ מֶלֶךְ הָעוֹלָם, אֲשֶׁר קִדְּשָׁנוּ בְּמִצְוֹתָיו, וְצִוָּנוּ לְהַדְלִיק נֵר שֶׁל (בשבת: שַׁבָּת וְשֶׁל) יוֹם הַכִּיפּוּרִים.

Baruch ata Adonai Elohenu melech ha'olam asher kidshanu bemitzvotav vetzivanu l'hadlik ner shel (on Shabbat, add "shel shabbat veshel") yom ha-kippurim.

Praised are You Adonai our God Ruler of the Universe who has made us holy with mitzvot and commanded us to light the candles of (Shabbat and) the Day of Atonement.

Hanukkah Blessings

57.

בָּרוּךְ אַתָּה יְיָ אֱלֹהֵינוּ מֶלֶךְ הָעוֹלָם, אֲשֶׁר קִדְּשָׁנוּ בְּמִצְוֹתָיו, וְצִוָּנוּ לְהַדְלִיק נֵר שֶׁל חֲנֻכָּה.

Baruch ata Adonai Elohenu melech haʼolam asher kidshanu bemitzvotav vetzivanu lʼhadlik ner shel Hanukkah.

Praised are You Adonai our God Ruler of the Universe who has made us holy with mitzvot and commanded us to light the Hanukkah candles.

58.

בָּרוּךְ אַתָּה יְיָ אֱלֹהֵינוּ מֶלֶךְ הָעוֹלָם, שֶׁעָשָׂה נִסִּים לַאֲבוֹתֵינוּ בַּיָּמִים הָהֵם בַּזְּמַן הַזֶּה.

Baruch ata Adonai Elohenu melech ha'olam she'asah nisim l'avotaynu ba-yamim hahaym bazman hazeh.

Praised are You Adonai our God Ruler of the Universe who accomplished miracles for our ancestors in ancient days, and in our time.

Passover Haggadah Blessings

59.

בָּרוּךְ אַתָּה יְיָ, אֱלֹהֵינוּ מֶלֶךְ הָעוֹלָם, בּוֹרֵא פְּרִי
הַגָּפֶן:

Baruch ata Adonai Elohenu melech haʼolam boray pri ha-gafen.

Praised are You, Adonai our God, Ruler of the Universe, who creates fruit of the vine.

60.

בָּרוּךְ אַתָּה יְיָ אֱלֹהֵינוּ מֶלֶךְ הָעוֹלָם, אֲשֶׁר קִדְּשָׁנוּ
בְּמִצְוֹתָיו, וְצִוָּנוּ עַל אֲכִילַת מָרוֹר:

*Baruch ata Adonai Elohenu melech ha'olam asher
kidshanu bemitzvotav vetzeevanu al acheelat
maror.*

Praised are You, Adonai our God, Ruler of the
Universe, who has made us holy with mitzvot and
commanded us concerning the eating of bitter
herbs.

61.

בָּרוּךְ אַתָּה יְיָ, אֱלֹהֵינוּ מֶלֶךְ הָעוֹלָם, אֲשֶׁר קִדְּשָׁנוּ בְּמִצְוֹתָיו, וְצִוָּנוּ עַל אֲכִילַת מַצָּה:

Baruch ata Adonai Elohenu melech ha'olam asher kidshanu bemitzvotav vetzeevanu al acheelat matzah.

Praised are You, Adonai our God, Ruler of the Universe, who has made us holy by mitzvot and commanded us to observe the eating of matzah.

Blessings after the Meal

62.

בָּרוּךְ אַתָּה יְיָ, אֱלֹהֵינוּ מֶלֶךְ הָעוֹלָם, הַזָּן אֶת
הָעוֹלָם כֻּלּוֹ בְּטוּבוֹ בְּחֵן בְּחֶסֶד וּבְרַחֲמִים הוּא נוֹתֵן
לֶחֶם לְכָל בָּשָׂר כִּי לְעוֹלָם חַסְדּוֹ. וּבְטוּבוֹ הַגָּדוֹל
תָּמִיד לֹא חָסַר לָנוּ, וְאַל יֶחְסַר לָנוּ מָזוֹן לְעוֹלָם
וָעֶד. בַּעֲבוּר שְׁמוֹ הַגָּדוֹל, כִּי הוּא אֵל זָן וּמְפַרְנֵס
לַכֹּל וּמֵטִיב לַכֹּל, וּמֵכִין מָזוֹן לְכֹל בְּרִיּוֹתָיו אֲשֶׁר
בָּרָא. בָּרוּךְ אַתָּה יְיָ, הַזָּן אֶת הַכֹּל:

Baruch ata Adonai Elohenu melech ha'olam
hazan et ha'olam kulo be-tuvo bechayn bechesed
u'vrachameem hu notayn lechem lechol basar kee
l'olam chasdo uv'tuvo ha-gadol tameed lo chasar lanu
ve'al yechsar lanu mazon le'olam va'ed ba'avur shemo
ha-gadol kee hu zan um'farnays lakol u'mayteev

*lakol u'maycheen mazon lechol be-reeyotav asher
bara. Baruch ata Adonai hazan et ha-kol.*

Praised are You, Adonai our God, Ruler of the
Universe, graciously sustaining the whole world
with kindness and compassion, providing food for
every creature, for God's love endures forever. God,
abounding in kindness, has never failed us. May
our nourishment be assured forever. God sustains
all life and is good to all, providing every creature
with food and sustenance. We praise You, Adonai,
who sustains all life.

63.

בָּרוּךְ אַתָּה יְיָ, עַל הָאָרֶץ וְעַל הַמָּזוֹן:

Baruch ata Adonai al ha'aretz ve'al ha-mazon

Praised are You, Adonai, for the land and for
sustenance.

64.

בָּרוּךְ אַתָּה יְיָ, בּוֹנֶה בְּרַחֲמָיו יְרוּשָׁלָיִם. אָמֵן.

Baruch ata Adonai boneh ve-rachamav ye-rushalayim amen.

Praised are You, Adonai, who in mercy rebuilds Jerusalem, Amen.

Haftorah Blessings

(Before the Haftarah)

65.

בָּרוּךְ אַתָּה יְיָ אֱלֹהֵינוּ מֶלֶךְ הָעוֹלָם, אֲשֶׁר בָּחַר
בִּנְבִיאִים טוֹבִים, וְרָצָה בְדִבְרֵיהֶם הַנֶּאֱמָרִים
בֶּאֱמֶת, בָּרוּךְ אַתָּה יְיָ, הַבּוֹחֵר בַּתּוֹרָה וּבְמֹשֶׁה
עַבְדּוֹ, וּבְיִשְׂרָאֵל עַמּוֹ, וּבִנְבִיאֵי הָאֱמֶת וָצֶדֶק.

*Baruch ata Adonai Elohenu melech ha'olam
asher bachar been'vee-yeem toveem ve-ratzah
vedeevrayhem ha-ne-emareem be-emet. Baruch ata
Adonai ha-bocher batorah uv-Moshe avdo uv'yisrael
amo un'veeyay ha'emet va-tzedek.*

Praised are You, Adonai our God, who rules the
universe, appointing devoted prophets and uphold-
ing their teachings, messages of truth. Praised are
You, Adonai, who loves the Torah, Moses His
servant, Israel His people, and prophets of truth
and righteousness.

66.

בָּרוּךְ אַתָּה יְיָ אֱלֹהֵינוּ מֶלֶךְ הָעוֹלָם, צוּר כָּל
הָעוֹלָמִים, צַדִּיק בְּכָל הַדּוֹרוֹת...בָּרוּךְ אַתָּה יְיָ,
הָאֵל הַנֶּאֱמָן בְּכָל דְּבָרָיו.

Baruch ata Adonai Elohenu melech ha'olam tzur kol
ha'olameem tzadeek bechol ha-dorot...Baruch ata
Adonai ha'El ha'ne'eman bechol devarav.

Praised are You, Adonai our God, who rules the
universe, Rock of all ages, righteous in all genera-
tions...Praised are You, Adonai, faithful in all Your
promises.

67.

רַחֵם עַל צִיּוֹן...בָּרוּךְ אַתָּה יְיָ, מְשַׂמֵּחַ צִיּוֹן בְּבָנֶיהָ.

Rachem al tziyon...Baruch ata Adonai me'same'ach
tziyon bi-vaneha.

Show compassion for Zion...Praised are You,
Adonai, who brings joy to Zion.

68.

שַׂמְּחֵנוּ יְיָ אֱלֹהֵינוּ בְּאֵלִיָּהוּ הַנָּבִיא עַבְדֶּךָ...בָּרוּךְ
אַתָּה יְיָ, מָגֵן דָּוִד.

*Samchaynu Adonai Elohenu be'Eliyahu ha-navi
avdecha...Baruch ata Adonai magen David.*

Bring us joy, Adonai our God, through Your
prophet Elijah... Praised are You, Adonai, Shield
of David.

69.

עַל הַתּוֹרָה, וְעַל הָעֲבוֹדָה, וְעַל הַנְּבִיאִים...בָּרוּךְ
אַתָּה יְיָ, מְקַדֵּשׁ הַשַּׁבָּת.

*Al ha-Torah ve'al ha'avodah ve'al han-veeyeem...
Baruch ata Adonai mekadesh ha-shabbat.*

We thank You and praise You, Adonai our God for
the Torah, for worship, for the prophets. Praised
are You Adonai who sanctifies the Sabbath.

Food Blessings

୬ BREAD

70.

בָּרוּךְ אַתָּה יְיָ, אֱלֹהֵינוּ מֶלֶךְ הָעוֹלָם, הַמּוֹצִיא לֶחֶם מִן הָאָרֶץ:

Baruch ata Adonai Elohenu melech ha'olam hamotzi lechem min ha'aretz.

Praised are You, Adonai our God, Ruler of the Universe who brings forth bread from the earth.

71.

בָּרוּךְ אַתָּה יְיָ אֱלֹהֵינוּ מֶלֶךְ הָעוֹלָם, אֲשֶׁר קִדְּשָׁנוּ
בְּמִצְוֹתָיו, וְצִוָּנוּ לְהַפְרִישׁ חַלָּה.

*Baruch ata Adonai Elohenu melech ha'olam asher
kidshanu bemitzvotav vetzeevanu lehafreesh
challah*

Praised are You, Adonai our God, Ruler of the
Universe, whose mitzvot add holiness to our lives
and who commanded us to separate the challah.

♬ FOOD (OTHER THAN BREAD) PREPARED
   FROM WHEAT, BARLEY, RYE, OATS OR SPELT.

72.

בָּרוּךְ אַתָּה יְיָ אֱלֹהֵינוּ מֶלֶךְ הָעוֹלָם, בּוֹרֵא מִינֵי
מְזוֹנוֹת.

*Baruch ata Adonai Elohenu melech ha'olam boray
meenay mezonote.*

Praised are You, Adonai our God, Ruler of the Universe who creates various kinds of nourishment.

♬ WINE OR GRAPE JUICE

73.

בָּרוּךְ אַתָּה יְיָ, אֱלֹהֵינוּ מֶלֶךְ הָעוֹלָם, בּוֹרֵא פְּרִי
הַגָּפֶן:

*Baruch ata Adonai Elohenu melech ha'olam boray
pri ha-gafen.*

Praised are You, Adonai our God, Ruler of the
Universe, who creates fruit of the vine.

74.

בָּרוּךְ אַתָּה יְיָ אֱלֹהֵינוּ מֶלֶךְ הָעוֹלָם, בּוֹרֵא פְרִי הָעֵץ.

Baruch ata Adonai Elohenu melech ha'olam boray pri ha'etz.

Praised are You, Adonai our God, Ruler of the Universe, who creates fruit of the tree.

75.

בָּרוּךְ אַתָּה יְיָ אֱלֹהֵינוּ מֶלֶךְ הָעוֹלָם, שֶׁהֶחֱיָנוּ וְקִיְּמָנוּ וְהִגִּיעָנוּ לַזְּמַן הַזֶּה.

Baruch ata Adonai Elohenu melech ha'olam she-he-cheyanu ve-kimanu ve-heegeeyanu lazman hazeh.

Praised are You, Adonai our God, Ruler of the Universe, for granting us life, for sustaining us, and for helping us to reach this day.

76.

בָּרוּךְ אַתָּה יְיָ, אֱלֹהֵינוּ מֶלֶךְ הָעוֹלָם, בּוֹרֵא פְּרִי הָאֲדָמָה:

Baruch ata Adonai Elohenu melech ha'olam boray pri ha-adamah.

Praised are You, Adonai our God, Ruler of the Universe who creates fruit of the ground.

❧ OTHER FOOD AND DRINK

77.

בָּרוּךְ אַתָּה יְיָ אֱלֹהֵינוּ מֶלֶךְ הָעוֹלָם, שֶׁהַכֹּל נִהְיֶה בִּדְבָרוֹ.

Baruch ata Adonai Elohenu melech ha'olam she-hakol nihyeh beedvaro.

Praised are You, Adonai our God, Ruler of the Universe at whose word all things come into being.

Havdalah Blessings

78.

בָּרוּךְ אַתָּה יְיָ אֱלֹהֵינוּ מֶלֶךְ הָעוֹלָם, בּוֹרֵא פְּרִי
הַגָּפֶן.

*Baruch ata Adonai Elohenu melech ha'olam boray
pri ha-gafen.*

Praised are You, Adonai our God, Ruler of the
Universe who creates the fruit of the vine.

79.

בָּרוּךְ אַתָּה יְיָ, אֱלֹהֵינוּ מֶלֶךְ הָעוֹלָם, בּוֹרֵא מִינֵי
בְשָׂמִים:

*Baruch ata Adonai Elohenu melech ha'olam boray
meenay besameem.*

Praised are You, Adonai our God, Ruler of the
universe, who creates many kinds of spices.

❧ OVER THE LIGHT OF THE HAVDALAH
   CANDLE

80.

בָּרוּךְ אַתָּה יְיָ, אֱלֹהֵינוּ מֶלֶךְ הָעוֹלָם, בּוֹרֵא מְאוֹרֵי
הָאֵשׁ:

*Baruch ata Adonai Elohenu melech ha'olam boray
me'oray ha'aysh.*

Praised are You, Adonai our God, Ruler of the
Universe, who creates the lights of the fire.

84.

בָּרוּךְ אַתָּה יְיָ אֱלֹהֵינוּ מֶלֶךְ הָעוֹלָם, בּוֹרֵא עִשְׂבֵי
בְשָׂמִים.

*Baruch ata Adonai Elohenu melech ha'olam boray
eesvay vesameem.*

Praised are You, Adonai our God, Ruler of the
Universe who creates fragrant plants.

☞ UPON SMELLING FRAGRANT FRUIT

85.

בָּרוּךְ אַתָּה יְיָ אֱלֹהֵינוּ מֶלֶךְ הָעוֹלָם, הַנּוֹתֵן רֵיחַ טוֹב
בַּפֵּרוֹת.

*Baruch ata Adonai Elohenu melech ha'olam ha-
noten rei-ach tov ba-perot.*

Praised are You, Adonai our God, Ruler of the
Universe, who gives a pleasant fragrance to fruits.

בָּרוּךְ אַתָּה יְיָ, אֱלֹהֵינוּ מֶלֶךְ הָעוֹלָם, הַמַּבְדִּיל בֵּין
קֹדֶשׁ לְחוֹל, בֵּין אוֹר לְחֹשֶׁךְ, בֵּין יִשְׂרָאֵל לָעַמִּים,
בֵּין יוֹם הַשְּׁבִיעִי, לְשֵׁשֶׁת יְמֵי הַמַּעֲשֶׂה: בָּרוּךְ אַתָּה
יְיָ, הַמַּבְדִּיל בֵּין קֹדֶשׁ לְחוֹל:

*Baruch ata Adonai Elohenu melech ha'olam ha-
mavdil bayn kodesh le-chol bayn or le-choshech
bayn yisrael la-a-meem bayn yom ha-shevi'i le-
sheshet yemay ha-ma'aseh. Baruch ata Adonai ha-
mavdil bayn kodesh lechol.*

Praised are You, Adonai our God, Ruler of the Universe, who has endowed all creation with distinc-
tive qualities, distinguishing between sacred and
secular time, between light and darkness, between
the people of Israel and other people, between
the seventh day and the six working days of the
week. Praised are You, Adonai, who distinguishes
between sacred and secular time.

Prayers for Various Occasions

82.

בָּרוּךְ אַתָּה יְיָ, אֱלֹהֵינוּ מֶלֶךְ הָעוֹלָם, בּוֹרֵא מִינֵי בְשָׂמִים:

Baruch ata Adonai Elohenu melech ha'olam boray meenay besameem.

Praised are You, Adonai our God, Ruler of the Universe who creates various spices.

UPON SMELLING THE FRAGRANCE OF T
OR SHRUBS

83.

אַתָּה יְיָ אֱלֹהֵינוּ מֶלֶךְ הָעוֹלָם, בּוֹרֵא עֲצֵי
ם.

Baruch ata Adonai Elohenu melech ha'olan atzay vesameem.

Praised are You, Adonai our God, Rule
Universe who creates fragrant trees.

86.

בָּרוּךְ אַתָּה יְיָ אֱלֹהֵינוּ מֶלֶךְ הָעוֹלָם, בּוֹרֵא שֶׁמֶן
עָרֵב.

Baruch ata Adonai Elohenu melech ha'olam boray shemen arayv.

Praised are You, Adonai our God, Ruler of the Universe, who creates fragrant oil.

87.

בָּרוּךְ אַתָּה יְיָ אֱלֹהֵינוּ מֶלֶךְ הָעוֹלָם, עֹשֶׂה מַעֲשֵׂה
בְרֵאשִׁית.

*Baruch ata Adonai Elohenu melech ha'olam oseh
ma'aseh veraysheet.*

Praised are You, Adonai our God, Ruler of the
Universe, Source of Creation.

88.

בָּרוּךְ אַתָּה יְיָ אֱלֹהֵינוּ מֶלֶךְ הָעוֹלָם, שֶׁכֹּחוֹ וּגְבוּרָתוֹ מָלֵא עוֹלָם.

Baruch ata Adonai Elohenu melech ha'olam she-kocho u'gevurato malay olam.

Praised are You, Adonai our God, Ruler of the Universe, whose power and might fill the world.

89.

בָּרוּךְ אַתָּה יְיָ אֱלֹהֵינוּ מֶלֶךְ הָעוֹלָם, זוֹכֵר הַבְּרִית
וְנֶאֱמָן בִּבְרִיתוֹ וְקַיָּם בְּמַאֲמָרוֹ.

Baruch ata Adonai Elohenu melech ha'olam zocher ha-berit ve-ne'eman b'eevreeto vekayam be-ma-amaro.

Praised are You, Adonai our God, Ruler of the Universe, who remembers His covenant, is faithful to it, and keeps His promise.

90.

בָּרוּךְ אַתָּה יְיָ אֱלֹהֵינוּ מֶלֶךְ הָעוֹלָם, שֶׁלֹּא חִסַּר בְּעוֹלָמוֹ דָּבָר, וּבָרָא בוֹ בְּרִיּוֹת טוֹבוֹת וְאִילָנוֹת טוֹבִים לְהַנּוֹת בָּהֶם בְּנֵי אָדָם.

Baruch ata Adonai Elohenu melech ha'olam shelo chisar b'olamo davar, u-vara vo briyot tovot v'ilanot tovim l'hanot bahem b'nai adam.

Praised are You, Adonai our God, Ruler of the Universe, who has withheld nothing from His world and who has created beautiful creatures and beautiful trees for people to enjoy.

91.

בָּרוּךְ אַתָּה יְיָ אֱלֹהֵינוּ מֶלֶךְ הָעוֹלָם, שֶׁעָשָׂה אֶת־
הַיָּם הַגָּדוֹל.

*Baruch ata Adonai Elohenu melech ha'olam she-
asah et hayam ha-gadol.*

Praised are You, Adonai our God, Ruler of the
Universe, who has made the great sea.

☙ UPON SEEING TREES OR CREATURES OF
STRIKING BEAUTY

92.

בָּרוּךְ אַתָּה יְיָ אֱלֹהֵינוּ מֶלֶךְ הָעוֹלָם, שֶׁכָּכָה לוֹ
בְּעוֹלָמוֹ.

*Baruch ata Adonai Elohenu melech ha'olam she-
kacha lo b'olamo.*

Praised are You, Adonai our God, Ruler of the
Universe who has such beauty in His world.

93.

בָּרוּךְ אַתָּה יְיָ אֱלֹהֵינוּ מֶלֶךְ הָעוֹלָם, שֶׁחָלַק
מֵחָכְמָתוֹ לִירֵאָיו.

*Baruch ata Adonai Elohenu melech ha'olam she-
chalak mee-chachmato liray-av.*

Praised are You, Adonai our God, Ruler of the
Universe, who has shared of His wisdom with
those who revere Him.

94.

בָּרוּךְ אַתָּה יְיָ אֱלֹהֵינוּ מֶלֶךְ הָעוֹלָם, שֶׁנָּתַן מֵחָכְמָתוֹ
לְבָשָׂר וָדָם.

*Baruch ata Adonai Elohenu melech ha'olam she-
natan mee-chochmato l'vasar va-dam.*

Praised are You, Adonai our God, Ruler of the
Universe who has given of His wisdom to flesh
and blood.

95.

בָּרוּךְ אַתָּה יְיָ אֱלֹהֵינוּ מֶלֶךְ הָעוֹלָם, שֶׁחָלַק מִכְּבוֹדוֹ לְבָשָׂר וָדָם.

Baruch ata Adonai Elohenu melech ha'olam she-natan meekvodo le-vasar va-dam.

Praised are You, Adonai our God, Ruler of the Universe, who has given of His glory to flesh and blood.

☙ UPON HEARING GOOD NEWS

96.

בָּרוּךְ אַתָּה יְיָ אֱלֹהֵינוּ מֶלֶךְ הָעוֹלָם, הַטּוֹב וְהַמֵּטִיב.

Baruch ata Adonai Elohenu melech ha'olam ha-tov v'ha-mayteev.

Praised are You, Adonai our God, Ruler of the Universe, who is good and beneficent.

97.

בָּרוּךְ אַתָּה יְיָ אֱלֹהֵינוּ מֶלֶךְ הָעוֹלָם, דַּיַּן הָאֱמֶת.

Baruch ata Adonai Elohenu melech ha'olam dayan ha-emet.

Praised are You, Adonai our God, Ruler of the Universe, the true Judge.

98.

בָּרוּךְ אַתָּה יְיָ אֱלֹהֵינוּ מֶלֶךְ הָעוֹלָם, שֶׁעָשָׂה לִי נֵס בַּמָּקוֹם הַזֶּה.

Baruch ata Adonai Elohenu melech ha'olam she-asah lee nes ba-makom ha-zeh.

Praised are You, Adonai our God, Ruler of the Universe, who granted me a miracle in this place.

ᔆ UPON ATTACHING A MEZUZAH TO A DOORPOST

99.

בָּרוּךְ אַתָּה יְיָ אֱלֹהֵינוּ מֶלֶךְ הָעוֹלָם, אֲשֶׁר קִדְּשָׁנוּ
בְּמִצְוֹתָיו, וְצִוָּנוּ לִקְבּוֹעַ מְזוּזָה.

Baruch ata Adonai Elohenu melech ha'olam asher kidshanu bemitzvotav vetzivanu lik'bo'ah mezuzah.

Praised are You, Adonai our God, Ruler of the Universe, whose mitzvot add holiness to our lives and who gave us the mitzvah to attach mezuzot.

ᘓ UPON WEARING NEW CLOTHES OR USING
SOMETHING NEW FOR THE FIRST TIME.

100.

בָּרוּךְ אַתָּה יְיָ, אֱלֹהֵינוּ מֶלֶךְ הָעוֹלָם, שֶׁהֶחֱיָנוּ
וְקִיְּמָנוּ וְהִגִּיעָנוּ לַזְּמַן הַזֶּה:

*Baruch ata Adonai Elohenu melech ha'olam she-
he-cheyanu ve-keemanu ve-heegeeyanu lazman
hazeh.*

Praised are You, Adonai our God, Ruler of the
Universe for granting us life, for sustaining us and
for helping us to reach this day.

✌ UPON RECOVERING FROM SERIOUS ILLNESS OR RETURNING SAFELY FROM A LONG JOURNEY

101.

בָּרוּךְ אַתָּה יְיָ אֱלֹהֵינוּ מֶלֶךְ הָעוֹלָם, הַגּוֹמֵל לְחַיָּבִים טוֹבוֹת, שֶׁגְּמָלַנִי כָּל טוֹב:

Baruch ata Adonai Elohenu melech ha'olam ha-gomel l-chayaveem tovot she-g'malanee kol tov.

Praised are You, Adonai our God, Ruler of the Universe, who graciously bestows favor upon the undeserving, even as He has bestowed favor upon me.

102.

יְהִי רָצוֹן מִלְּפָנֶיךָ יְיָ אֱלֹהֵינוּ וֵאלֹהֵי אֲבוֹתֵינוּ,
שֶׁתּוֹלִיכֵנוּ לְשָׁלוֹם וְתַצְעִידֵנוּ לְשָׁלוֹם...בָּרוּךְ אַתָּה
יְיָ, שׁוֹמֵעַ תְּפִלָּה.

*Yehi ratzon meelefanecha Adonai Elohenu vaylohay
Avotaynu she-to-leechaynee leshalom ve'tatzeedanee
l'shalom...Baruch ata Adonai shomaya tefillah*

May it be Your will Adonai our God and God of
our ancestors, to guide us and sustain us in peace...
Praised are You, Adonai, who hears prayer.

103.

בָּרוּךְ אַתָּה יְיָ אֱלֹהֵינוּ מֶלֶךְ הָעוֹלָם, אֲשֶׁר קִדְּשָׁנוּ
בְּמִצְוֹתָיו, וְצִוָּנוּ עַל סְפִירַת הָעֹמֶר.

*Baruch ata Adonai Elohenu melech ha'olam asher
kidshanu bemitzvotav vetzeevanu al sefirat ha-
omer.*

Praised are You, Adonai our God, Ruler of the Universe, whose mitzvot add holiness to our lives and
who gave us the mitzvah of counting the Omer.

104.

בָּרוּךְ אַתָּה יְיָ אֱלֹהֵינוּ מֶלֶךְ הָעוֹלָם, אֲשֶׁר קִדְּשָׁנוּ
בְּמִצְוֹתָיו, וְצִוָּנוּ עַל נְטִילַת לוּלָב.

Baruch ata Adonai Elohenu melech ha'olam asher
kidshanu bemitzvotav vetzeevanu al nitilat lulav.

Praised are You, Adonai our God, Ruler of the
Universe whose mitzvot add holiness to our lives
and who gave us the mitzvah to take up the lulav.

105.

בָּרוּךְ אַתָּה יְיָ אֱלֹהֵינוּ מֶלֶךְ הָעוֹלָם, אֲשֶׁר קִדְּשָׁנוּ בְּמִצְוֹתָיו, וְצִוָּנוּ לִקְרֹא אֶת הַהַלֵּל.

Baruch ata Adonai Elohenu melech haolam asher kidshanu bemitzvotav vetzeevanu leekro et hahallel.

Praised are You, Adonai our God, Ruler of the Universe whose mitzvot add holiness to our lives and who gave us the mitzvah to recite Hallel.

106.

בָּרוּךְ אַתָּה יְיָ אֱלֹהֵינוּ מֶלֶךְ הָעוֹלָם, אֲשֶׁר קִדְּשָׁנוּ בְּמִצְוֹתָיו, וְצִוָּנוּ עַל בִּעוּר חָמֵץ.

Baruch ata Adonai Elohenu melech ha'olam asher kidshanu bemitzvotav vetzeevanu al bi'ur chametz

Praised are You, Adonai our God, Ruler of the universe whose mitzvot add holiness to our lives and who commanded us to search for leaven.

107.

בָּרוּךְ אַתָּה יְיָ אֱלֹהֵינוּ מֶלֶךְ הָעוֹלָם, אֲשֶׁר קִדְּשָׁנוּ בְּמִצְוֹתָיו, וְצִוָּנוּ עַל מִקְרָא מְגִלָּה.

Baruch ata Adonai Elohenu melech ha'olam asher kidshanu bemitzvotav vetzeevanu al meekra megillah.

Praised are You, Adonai our God, Ruler of the Universe who has made us holy with mitzvot and commanded us concerning the reading of the Megillah.

108.

בָּרוּךְ אַתָּה יְיָ אֱלֹהֵינוּ מֶלֶךְ הָעוֹלָם, אֲשֶׁר קִדְּשָׁנוּ בְּמִצְוֹתָיו, וְצִוָּנוּ לֵישֵׁב בַּסֻּכָּה.

Baruch ata Adonai Elohenu melech ha'olam asher kidshanu bemitzvotav vetzeevanu layshev basukkah.

Praised are You, Adonai our God, Ruler of the Universe, who has made us holy by mitzvot and commanded us to dwell in a Sukkah.

Life Cycle Blessings

109.

בָּרוּךְ אַתָּה יְיָ אֱלֹהֵינוּ מֶלֶךְ הָעוֹלָם, אֲשֶׁר קִדְּשָׁנוּ בְּמִצְוֹתָיו, וְצִוָּנוּ עַל הַמִּילָה.

Baruch ata Adonai Elohenu melech ha'olam asher kidshanu bemitzvotav vetzeevanu al ha-milah.

Praised are You, Adonai our God, Ruler of the Universe, who has made us holy with mitzvot and commanded us concerning the ritual of circumcision.

110.

בָּרוּךְ אַתָּה יְיָ אֱלֹהֵינוּ מֶלֶךְ הָעוֹלָם, אֲשֶׁר קִדְּשָׁנוּ בְּמִצְוֹתָיו, וְצִוָּנוּ לְהַכְנִיסוֹ בִּבְרִיתוֹ שֶׁל אַבְרָהָם אָבִינוּ.

Baruch ata Adonai Elohenu melech ha'olam asher kidshanu bemitzvotav vetzivanu le'hachneeso beevreeto shel Avraham avinu.

Praised are You, Adonai our God, Ruler of the Universe, who has made us holy with mitzvot and has commanded us to bring him into the covenant of Abraham our forefather.

111.

בָּרוּךְ אַתָּה יְיָ אֱלֹהֵינוּ מֶלֶךְ הָעוֹלָם, אֲשֶׁר קִדְּשָׁנוּ
בְּמִצְוֹתָיו, וְצִוָּנוּ עַל פִּדְיוֹן הַבֵּן.

*Baruch ata Adonai Elohenu melech ha'olam asher
kidshanu bemitzvotav vetzeevanu al pidyon ha-
ben.*

Praised are You, Adonai our God, Ruler of the
Universe, who has made us holy by mitzvot and
commanded us concerning the redemption of the
first born.

112.

בָּרוּךְ אַתָּה יְיָ, אֱלֹהֵינוּ מֶלֶךְ הָעוֹלָם, בּוֹרֵא פְּרִי
הַגָּפֶן:

Baruch ata Adonai Elohenu melech ha'olam boray pri ha-gafen.

Praised are You, Adonai, Ruler of the Universe, who creates the fruit of the vine.

113.

בָּרוּךְ אַתָּה יְיָ אֱלֹהֵינוּ מֶלֶךְ הָעוֹלָם, שֶׁהַכֹּל בָּרָא
לִכְבוֹדוֹ.

Baruch ata Adonai Elohenu melech ha'olam she-hakol barah leechvodo.

Praised are You, Adonai, Ruler of the Universe, who created all things for Your glory.

בָּרוּךְ אַתָּה יְיָ אֱלֹהֵינוּ מֶלֶךְ הָעוֹלָם, יוֹצֵר הָאָדָם.

Baruch ata Adonai Elohenu melech ha'olam yotzer ha'adam.

Praised are You, Adonai, Ruler of the Universe, Creator of human beings.

בָּרוּךְ אַתָּה יְיָ אֱלֹהֵינוּ מֶלֶךְ הָעוֹלָם, אֲשֶׁר יָצַר אֶת הָאָדָם בְּצַלְמוֹ, בְּצֶלֶם דְּמוּת תַּבְנִיתוֹ, וְהִתְקִין לוֹ מִמֶּנּוּ בִּנְיָן עֲדֵי עַד. בָּרוּךְ אַתָּה יְיָ, יוֹצֵר הָאָדָם.

Baruch ata Adonai Elohenu melech ha'olalm asher yatzar et ha-adam betzalmo betzelem demut tavneeto ve-heetkeen lo meemenu binyan aday ad. Baruch ata Adonai yotzer ha-adam.

Praised are You, Adonai our God, Ruler of the Universe, who creates man and woman in Your image, fashioning woman from man as his partner. Praised are You, Creator of human beings.

116.

שׂוֹשׂ תָּשִׂישׂ וְתָגֵל הָעֲקָרָה בְּקִבּוּץ בָּנֶיהָ לְתוֹכָהּ
בְּשִׂמְחָה. בָּרוּךְ אַתָּה יְיָ, מְשַׂמֵּחַ צִיּוֹן בְּבָנֶיהָ.

*Sos tasees ve-tagel ha'akarah bekeebutz bane-ha le-
tocha be-simcha. Baruch ata Adonai me-same'ach
tziyon bivane-ha.*

May Zion be happy as her children are restored to
joy. Praised are You, Adonai, who causes Zion to
be happy at her children's return.

117.

שַׂמֵּחַ תְּשַׂמַּח רֵעִים הָאֲהוּבִים כְּשַׂמֵּחֲךָ יְצִירְךָ בְּגַן
עֵדֶן מִקֶּדֶם. בָּרוּךְ אַתָּה יְיָ, מְשַׂמֵּחַ חָתָן וְכַלָּה.

Sameach te-samach re'im ha'ahuvim ke-samaychecha
yetzeercha began eden meekedem. Baruch ata
Adonai mesameach chatan ve-challah.

Grant perfect joy to these loving companions, as
You did to the first man and woman in the Garden
of Eden. Praised are You, Adonai, who grants happiness to bride and groom.

118.

בָּרוּךְ אַתָּה יְיָ אֱלֹהֵינוּ מֶלֶךְ הָעוֹלָם, אֲשֶׁר בָּרָא
שָׂשׂוֹן וְשִׂמְחָה, חָתָן וְכַלָּה, גִּילָה, רִנָּה, דִּיצָה
וְחֶדְוָה, אַהֲבָה וְאַחֲוָה וְשָׁלוֹם וְרֵעוּת. מְהֵרָה יְיָ
אֱלֹהֵינוּ יִשָּׁמַע בְּעָרֵי יְהוּדָה וּבְחֻצוֹת יְרוּשָׁלַיִם
קוֹל שָׂשׂוֹן וְקוֹל שִׂמְחָה, קוֹל חָתָן וְקוֹל כַּלָּה,

קוֹל מִצְהֲלוֹת חֲתָנִים מֵחֻפָּתָם וּנְעָרִים מִמִּשְׁתֵּה
נְגִינָתָם. בָּרוּךְ אַתָּה יְיָ, מְשַׂמֵּחַ חָתָן עִם הַכַּלָּה.

Baruch ata Adonai Elohenu melech ha'olam asher
bara sasson ve-simcha chatan ve-kallah gila rina
ditza ve-chedva ahavah vi-achva ve-shalom ve-rayut
meherah Adonai Elohenu yeeshama b'oray yehudah
u'vchutzot yerushalayim kol sasson vekol simcha
kol chatan vekol kallah kol meetzalot chataneem
maychupatam un-areem mee-mishteh negeenatam.
Baruch ata Adonai me-sameach chatan eem ha-
kallah.

Praised are You, Adonai our God, Ruler of the
Universe, who creates joy and gladness, bride
and groom, happiness, delight, rejoicing, love and
harmony, peace and friendship. May there be heard
in the cities of Judah and the streets of Jerusalem
voices of joy and happiness, bride and groom, the
jubilant voices of those joined in marriage under
the chuppah, the voices of young people feasting
and singing. Praised are You, Adonai, who causes
the groom to be happy with his bride.

119.

בָּרוּךְ אַתָּה יְיָ אֱלֹהֵינוּ מֶלֶךְ הָעוֹלָם, אֲשֶׁר קִדְּשָׁנוּ בְּמִצְוֹתָיו וְצִוָּנוּ עַל הַטְּבִילָה.

Baruch ata Adonai Elohenu melech haolam asher kidshanu bemitzvotav vetzeevanu al ha-tevillah.

Praised are You, Adonaii our God, Ruler of the Universe, whose mitzvot add holiness to our lives and who commanded us concerning ritual immersion.